Abram
and His Times

Lee W. Casperson

Copyright © 2020 Lee W. Casperson

All rights reserved. No part of this book may be used or reproduced by any means, graphic, electronic, or mechanical, including photocopying, recording, taping or by any information storage retrieval system without the written permission of the publisher except in the case of brief quotations embodied in critical articles and reviews.

Because of the dynamic nature of the Internet, any web addresses or links contained in this book may have changed since publication and may no longer be valid.

Published by Lee Casperson
Ewing, NJ 08638

ISBN: 978-1-7323189-2-2 (sc)

Library of Congress Control Number: 2020902210

Printed in the United States of America

Table Of Contents

LIST OF ILLUSTRATIONS……………..……………..vii

PREFACE…………………………..………………….ix

1. FROM NOAH TO ABRAM……………………………1

2. FROM TERAH TO THERA……………………………....9

3. WICKEDNESS OF SODOM……………………..… 23

4. DESTRUCTION OF SODOM AND GEMORRAH………..39

5. SARAH HAS A BABY…………………………………..49

6. THREE ERUPTIONS OF THERA……………..……. 55

7. THE ASTEROID AND THE VOLCANO……………..…61

8. FREQUENCY OF ASTEROID IMPACTS………………... 65

LIST OF ILLUSTRATIONS

Tables

Table 1. Biblical chronology of the patriarchs from Noah to Abram. The numbers shown are the ages of these patriarchs at the births of some of their biblically most important sons... 2

Table 2. Approximate biblical chronology for the period from Noah to Abram. The Biblical Age column corresponds to the Masoretic ages as given in Table 1. The column Adjusted Age indicates the approximate ages of the patriarchs at the births of their sons. The column Date indicates (except for the flood line) the dates of birth of those sons... 4

Table 3. Anatolian dendrochronology in relative tree-ring numbers, calendar years B.C., and normalized tree-ring thickness for the time period around a major growth anomaly associated with an asteroid impact near the Dead Sea during the lifetime of Abraham.. 46

Table 4. Anatolian dendrochronology in relative tree-ring numbers, calendar years B.C., and normalized tree-ring thickness for the time period around a major growth anomaly during the lifetime of Jacob.. 57

Table 5. Anatolian dendrochronology in relative tree-ring numbers, calendar years B.C., and normalized tree-ring thickness for the time period around a growth anomaly during the lifetime of Isaac... 58

Table 6. Anatolian dendrochronology in relative tree-ring numbers, calendar years B.C., and normalized tree-ring thickness for the time period around a growth anomaly during the lifetime of Abram...................................... 59

Figures

Figure 1. Map of Abram's major travels……………….………... 8

Figure 2. Sculpture entitled "Lot's Wife," created by Anna Mahler, 1904-1988……………………………………………….. 28

Figure 3. Relative tree-ring thickness for a growth anomaly in Anatolia that may be associated with an asteroid impact in the vicinity of the Dead Sea. The post-impact diminished growth period extended from at least 1704 B.C. to 1702 B.C. 48

PREFACE

Abram is one of the most important biblical personalities of the early Old Testament era. In spite of this importance, however, there is only limited plausible information about the chronology of his life. One of the purposes of this study is to develop a quantitative approach to the adventures and chronology of Abram's life. Thus, connections will be sought here between his activities and known events of history. While some of these connections may be precise, others are acknowledged to be better described as reasonable estimates.

There are several different methods by which one might attempt to establish the dates of events that occurred during the lifetime of Abram. As a first approach, one might try to connect the chronology of Abram's life to datable events that occurred before or after the time of Abram. The best known starting date for this method involves the date of Noah's flood. This date is thought to have been about 2035 B.C. based on tree-ring growth records from California. Similar but less precise values of this same flood date have been obtained from the climate records of China, Babylon, and Sumer. This event seems also to have been responsible for the extinction of the last mammoths on the earth.

The flooding noted above may have been caused by the impact on earth of an ice-bearing comet, and its date is associated with the most severe frost-ring occurrence in history. Frost-rings refer to narrowed or missing growth rings in trees that have been damaged by exceptionally cold weather, and dendrochronology (tree-ring dating) permits determination of the precise dates of the underlying frost events. Such frosts can be consequences of volcanic eruptions or comet impacts. Comets tend to originate in the cold outer areas of our solar system, and they may carry large volumes of water ice. In fact, water-carrying comets and asteroids have been recognized as major sources of the water that now exists on earth. More extreme and widespread climate disruptions, including especially flooding, may be associated with the occurrence in 2035 B.C. than with any other historical weather event.

Starting from the date of Noah's flood, various Bible-related chronological information can be employed to estimate the date of Abram's birth. Using his birth date and other biblical data one may then estimate the dates of important events in Abram's life. In that estimating process the Bible provides several checks on the dates that are obtained. Some of these checks are historical, relating to interactions of Abram and his family with other individuals and empires known to history. An example of this type would be Abram's rescue of his nephew Lot and his family and neighbors after they were taken captive from their homes in Sodom by a coalition of eastern kings.

Other checks relate to historically known geophysical events. Thus, the Bible in the book Genesis refers to three different famine events. The first of these occurred during the life of Abram, the second occurred during the life of Abram's son Isaac, and the third occurred during the life of Abram's grandson Jacob. These famines are each found to have been a consequence of an eruption of the volcano on the island of Thera. This eruption sequence is well known from geological studies, and the third of these eruptions was among the greatest volcanic events in history. The eruptions are datable from the tree-ring sequences in Anatolia, and they provide insights into the life chronologies of Abram, Isaac, and Jacob.

Another chronologically significant geophysical event associated with Abram involved the destruction of the biblical "cities of the plain" (Sodom, Gomorrah, Admah, and Zeboiim). This destruction was initiated by the impact of an asteroid in the vicinity of the Dead Sea, and the date of its occurrence is also evident in the Anatolian tree rings.

Acknowledgments

The author is pleased to acknowledge the guidance and encouragement provided many years ago by his parents on topics relating to the Bible and science. He is also appreciative of the assistance and patience of his wife Susan, son Robert, and daughter Janet in this and other projects.

1. FROM NOAH TO ABRAM

The purpose of this section is to develop a plausible chronology for times between Noah and Abram. There are important Bible stories relating to the time before Abram, and it is perhaps appropriate to focus initially on some of Abram's predecessors. For times after Abram and his family, the various fundamental versions of the Bible have fewer differences in chronology and fewer instances where the numbers given seem conspicuously doubtful. However, for the period from Noah to Abram, there are some basic concerns that must be addressed. The biblical data for this period are summarized in Table 1.[1]

Table 1. Biblical chronology of the patriarchs from Noah to Abram. The numbers shown are the ages of these patriarchs at the births of some of their biblically most important sons.

Patriarch	Verses	Masoretic	Samaritan	Septuagint
Noah	Genesis 5:32	502	502	502
Shem	Genesis 11:10	100	100	100
Arpachshad	Genesis 11:12	35	135	135
Kainan	Genesis 11:13	(30)		130
Shelah	Genesis 11:14	30	130	130
Eber	Genesis 11:16	34	134	134
Peleg	Genesis 11:18	30	130	130
Reu	Genesis 11:20	32	132	132
Serug	Genesis 11:22	30	130	130
Nahor	Genesis 11:24	29	79	79
Terah	Genesis 11:26	70	70	70
Abram	Genesis 16:16	86	86	86

One obvious problem with the information in the preceding table is that the various versions of the Bible sometimes disagree significantly with each other, and some intervals seem to be favored for these version differences. Thus, for the time from Arpachshad (the grandson of Noah) to Nahor (the grandfather of Abram), the ages of the patriarchs at the births of their principal successors are greater by exactly one hundred years (fifty years for Nahor) in the Samaritan and Septuagint versions of the Bible than in the more plausible Masoretic version. It is clear that to develop a useful and unique reference chronology, some assumptions are needed to address these and other discrepancies.

Since the Masoretic numbers for this period mostly seem more reasonable than those of the Samaritan and Septuagint texts (at least to the author), the Samaritan and Septuagint numbers will be discarded for this section of the chronology. Thus, the Masoretic numbers are considered first, supplemented initially by the number thirty (in parentheses) for the age of Kainan. It may be noticed that the Masoretic and Samaritan versions of the genealogy in Table 1 do not actually include Kainan, though he is present in the Septuagint (Genesis 11:13), the New Testament (Luke 3:36), and *The Book of Jubilees*[2] (Jubilees 8:1-5). The indicated Masoretic age of thirty years for Kainan is one hundred less than the Septuagint value of one hundred and thirty years, by analogy with the version differences of other names in this era that already have been mentioned.

Table 1 is only a relative chronology, as it contains no absolute dates. However, as noted in the opening paragraphs of the Preface above, Noah's flood is suggested to have occurred in the year 2035 B.C. This date can be used as a starting point to determine an approximate chronology for the period from the flood to Abram. The method is based primarily on the chronology of the Masoretic version of the Bible. As employed here, replacements are suggested for a few dates that seem conspicuously unrealistic, and the results are given as Table 2 below.

Table 2. Approximate biblical chronology for the period from Noah to Abram. The Biblical Age column corresponds to the Masoretic ages as given in Table 1. The column Adjusted Age indicates the approximate ages of the patriarchs at the births of their sons. The column Date indicates (except for the flood line) the dates of birth of those sons.

Patriarch	Biblical Age	Adjusted Age	Date
Noah	502	(31)	2064 B.C.
flood			2035
Shem	100	(31)	2033
Arpachshad	35	35	1998
Kainan	30	30	1968
Shelah	30	30	1938
Eber	34	34	1904
Peleg	30	30	1874
Reu	32	32	1842
Serug	30	30	1812
Nahor	29	29	1783
Terah	70	29	1754
Abram	86	36	1718

The people represented in this chronology/genealogy should perhaps be described as biblically significant sons (rather than most important or eldest sons). The implied son of Abram is Ishmael. The ages of most of the people in the table are from the biblical book Genesis and are associated with the patriarchs from

1. From Noah to Abram

Arpachshad to Nahor (supplemented by thirty years inferred from the Septuagint version for Kainan). These are the ages at the birth of a child, and they would probably not seem unreasonable, even in more modern times.

On the other hand, the best known people in the table are the first two (Noah and Shem) and the last two (Terah and Abram), and to enhance their significance they seem to have been assigned unreasonably high ages at the births of their sons. In this circumstance one can use the "reasonable" data in the table to approximate any unknown or seemingly unreasonable data in estimating multigenerational time intervals. The average of the ages of the eight patriarchs from Arpachshad to Nahor is about thirty-one years. Therefore, as a rationalization of the table, it is suggested that Shem may have been born when Noah was about thirty-one years old (rather than five hundred and two years old), and Arpachshad may have been born when Shem was about thirty-one years old (rather than one hundred years old). It is suggested from other considerations below that Terah may have been about twenty-nine years old when Abram was born in about 1754 B.C., and Abram may have been about thirty-six years old when his Egyptian wife Hagar gave birth to Ishmael in about 1718 B.C. With the modifications just summarized, an alternative approximate biblical chronology for the period from Noah to Abram is given in the fourth column of Table 2. In the table, the qualitatively-estimated thirty-one year intervals are included in parentheses in the Adjusted Age column for Noah and Shem. The calculated calendar year dates for the patriarchs from Noah to Abram at the births of their sons are included in the Date column.

The dates listed in Table 2 agree with the absolute dates that have been tentatively inferred in these investigations. Thus, the first line in the table suggests that Noah may have been about thirty-one years of age in 2064 B.C., when his son Shem was born. The first line could also suggest that Noah himself may have been born in about 2095 B.C., thirty-one years before Shem. Arpachshad is indicated to have been born in the year 2033 B.C. This number is consistent with the following biblical statement: "[Shem] became the father of Arpachshad two years after the flood" (Genesis 11:10). It follows that the date for Noah's flood is 2035 B.C. as identified previously. Thus, Noah was about *sixty years* old (2095-2035) at the onset of the flood rather than *six hundred years* old as indicated in Genesis 7:6,11.

Table 2 may be understood to suggest that Abram was born in approximately 1754 B.C., and his son Ishmael was born in approximately 1718 B.C. It remains now to identify other information that might help in confirming values for these and other dates. First, it may be recalled from Table 1 that the Septuagint age of Abram's grandfather Nahor is fifty years greater than his Masoretic age. This fifty-year discrepancy may also have affected (or infected) some of the other ages associated with the life of Abram, the grandson of Nahor. Thus, the reported occurrence of other events in Abram's life might also be excessively large by the amount of fifty years.

An approximate chronology of the Hebrews for the time of Abram's departure from Haran until the expulsion of the Hyksos from Egypt was given previously,[3] but that chronology did not include the destruction of Sodom. A more complete chronology of the Hebrews from the birth of Abram's father Terah to the

1. From Noah to Abram

eruption of Thera is included in Section 2 below. These dates are interconnected by means of the indicated verses from the Bible and other resources. Several fixed dates are provided by the known dates of such happenings as volcanic eruptions, famines, and the destruction of Sodom.

The path taken by Abram and his family following their departure from Ur is sketched on the map shown in Fig. 1 below. They traveled northwest from Ur to Haran where they remained until the death of Terah. Then Abram traveled south into Canaan with his family, while other descendants of Terah remained in Haran. With the occurrence of a severe famine in Canaan, Abram moved farther south into Egypt where he remained for several years before returning to Canaan. A more detailed summary of Abram's adventures and their chronology is included in the following section.

Abram and His Times

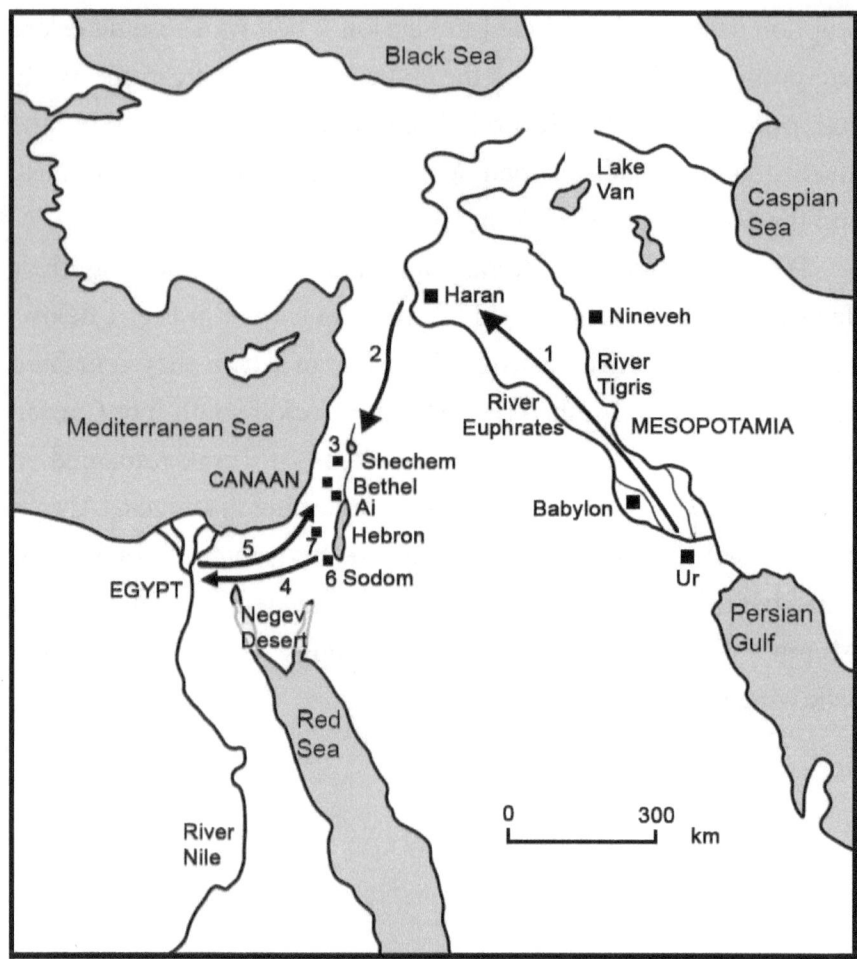

Figure 1. Map of Abram's major travels

2. FROM TERAH TO THERA

The purpose of this section is to provide a brief summary of many of the historical events for times from the birth of Abram's father Terah until the massive explosion of the volcano on the Mediterranean island of Thera. The first line in each of the following paragraph sections includes a title representing the main datable occurrence considered in the paragraph, followed by the age of Abram/Abraham when relevant, and then the date of the indicated occurrence. It is intended that many of these dates as amended are accurate almost to the year, but there are several instances of greater uncertainty. The following texts will generally reflect what seem to be relatively plausible statements from the Bible (RSV), Jasher,[4] or related literature concerning the events and the times of their occurrence. As with the Samaritan and Septuagint chronologies in Table 1, many (but not all) of the indicated ages in the notation of this section are assumed to be larger than the true ages by some simple integer number such as one hundred, fifty, or twenty, etc. Thus, numbers inserted in the text in brackets and accompanied by a question mark may be suggestive of the more probable values included in the calculations.

Abram and His Times

Subject	Age of Abram	Date
Nahor begat Terah		1783 B.C.

When Nahor had lived twenty-nine years, he became the father of Terah; and Nahor lived after the birth of Terah a hundred and nineteen [19?] years, and had other sons and daughters (Genesis 11:24-25).

[A]nd Nahor begat Terah, . . . (Jasher 7:22).

Terah took a wife

and begat Haran and Nahor   1765 B.C.

[A]nd Terah was thirty-eight [18?] years old, and he begat Haran and Nahor (Jasher 7:22).

Terah took a second wife

and begat Abram   0   1754 B.C.

And Terah took a [second] wife, and her name was Amthelo the daughter of Cornebo; and the wife of Terah conceived and bare him a son in those days. Terah was seventy [29?] years old when he begat him, and Terah called the name of his son that was born to him Abram, because the king had raised him in those days, and dignified him above all his princes that were with him (Jasher 7:50-51).

Haran begat Lot   8   1746 B.C.

And Haran, the son of Terah, Abram's oldest brother, took a wife in those days. Haran was thirty-nine [19?] years old when he took her; and the wife of Haran conceived and bare a son and he called his name Lot (Jasher 9:1-2).

2. From Terah to Thera

Haran begat Milca   9   1745 B.C.

And she conceived again and bare a daughter, and she called her name Milca; . . . (Jasher 9:3).

Haran begat Sarai   10   1744 B.C.

[A]nd she again conceived and bare a daughter, and she called her name Sarai. Haran was forty-two [21?] years old when he begat Sarai, which was in the tenth year of the life of Abram (Jasher 9:3-4).

Sodom rebelled against
Chedorlaomer (13 yrs in the past)   21   1733 B.C.

At that time [1720 B.C.] Chedorlaomer king of Elam sent to all the neighboring kings, to Nimrod king of Shinar who was then under his power, and to Tidal king of Goyim, and to Arioch king of Elasar, with whom he made a covenant, saying, come up to me and assist me, that we may smite all the towns of Sodom and its inhabitants, for they have rebelled against me these thirteen years [since 1733 B.C.] (Jasher 16:1).

Terah and Abram travel
from Ur to Haran   22   1732 B.C.

Terah took Abram his son and Lot the son of Haran, his grandson, and Sarai his daughter-in-law, his son Abram's wife, and they went forth together from Ur of the Chaldeans to go into the land of Canaan; but when they came to Haran, they settled there (Genesis 11:31).

And Terah took his son Abram and his grandson Lot, the son of Haran, and Sarai his daughter-in-law, the wife of his son Abram, and all the souls of his household and went with them from Ur Casdim to go to the land of Canaan.

Abram and His Times

And when they came as far as the land of Haran they remained there, . . . (Jasher 13:1).

Then he [Abram] departed from the land of the Chaldeans, and lived in Haran (Acts 7:4).

Death of Terah   24   1730 B.C.

The days of Terah were two hundred and five [53?] years; and Terah died in Haran. Now the Lord said to Abram, "Go from your country and your kindred and your father's house to the land that I will show you" (Genesis 11:32-12:1).

And the days of Terah were two hundred and five [53?] years, and he was buried in Haran (Jasher 22:34).

And after his father [Terah] died, God removed him [Abram] from there into this land [Canaan] in which you are now living (Acts 7:4).

[It is suggested that Abram remained in Haran as long as Terah was alive and migrated to Canaan shortly after Terah's death.]

Abram moves from
Haran to Canaan   25   1729 B.C.

So Abram went, as the Lord had told him; and Lot went with him. Abram was seventy-five [25?] years old when he departed from Haran. And Abram took Sarai his wife, and Lot his brother's son, and all their possessions which they had gathered, and the persons that they had gotten in Haran; and they set forth to go to the land of Canaan. When they had come to the land of Canaan, Abram passed through the land to the place at Shechem, to the oak of Moreh (Genesis 12:4-6).

2. From Terah to Thera

And Abram remained in the land [of Haran] three years, and at the expiration of three years the Lord appeared to Abram and said to him; I am the Lord who brought thee forth from Ur Casdim, and delivered thee from the hands of all thine enemies. . . . Arise now, take thy wife and all belonging to thee and go to the land of Canaan and remain there, and I will there be unto thee for a God, and I will bless thee. And Abram rose and took his wife and all belonging to him, and he went to the land of Canaan as the Lord had told him; and Abram was fifty [25?] years old when he went from Haran (Jasher 13:3, 5).

Famine in the land

(Abram's famine)   25   1729 B.C.

Now there was a famine in the land. So Abram went down to Egypt to sojourn there, for the famine was severe in the land (Genesis 12:10).

And in that year there was a heavy famine throughout the land of Canaan, and the inhabitants of the land could not remain on account of the famine for it was very grievous. And Abram and all belonging to him rose and went down to Egypt on account of the famine (Jasher 15:1-2).

Abram goes back to Canaan   32   1722 B.C.

So Abram went up from Egypt, he and his wife, and all that he had, and Lot with him, into the Negeb. . . . And he journeyed on from the Negeb as far as Bethel, to the place where his tent had been at the beginning, between Bethel and Ai, to the place where he had made an altar at the first. . . . (Genesis 13:1, 3).

And Abram arose, and he and all belonging to him went away from Egypt; and Pharaoh ordered some of his men to accompany him and all that went with him. And Abram

Abram and His Times

returned to the land of Canaan, to the place where he had made the altar, where he at first had pitched his tent (Jasher 15:33-34).

Lot goes to Sodom   33   1721 B.C.

Then Abram said to Lot, "Let there be no strife between you and me, and between your herdsmen and my herdsmen; for we are kinsmen. Is not the whole land before you? Separate yourself from me. If you take the left hand, then I will go to the right; or if you take the right hand, then I will go to the left." And Lot lifted up his eyes, and saw that the Jordan valley was well watered everywhere like the garden of the Lord [Garden of Eden], like the land of Egypt in the direction of Zoar; this was before the Lord destroyed Sodom and Gomorrah. So Lot chose for himself all the Jordan valley, and Lot journeyed east; thus they separated from each other. Abram dwelt in the land of Canaan, while Lot dwelt among the cities of the valley and moved his tent as far as Sodom. Now the men of Sodom were wicked, great sinners against the Lord (Genesis 13:8-13).

And when Abram had spoken all these words to Lot, then Lot arose and lifted up his eyes toward the plain of Jordan. And he saw that the whole of this place was well watered, and good for man as well as affording pasture for the cattle. And Lot went from Abram to that place, and he there pitched his tent and he dwelt in Sodom, and they were separated from each other (Jasher 15:44-46).

Lot captured, then
rescued by Abram   34   1720 B.C.

- So the enemy took all the goods of Sodom and Gomorrah, and all their provisions, and went their way; they also took Lot, the son of Abram's brother, who dwelt in Sodom, and his goods, and departed. Then one who had escaped came,

2. From Terah to Thera

and told Abram the Hebrew, who was living by the oaks of Mamre the Amorite, brother of Eshcol and of Aner; these were allies of Abram. When Abram heard that his kinsman had been taken captive, he led forth his trained men, born in his house, three hundred and eighteen of them, and went in pursuit as far as Dan. And he divided his forces against them by night, he and his servants, and routed them and pursued them to Hobah, north of Damascus. Then he brought back all the goods, and also brought back his kinsman Lot with his goods, and the women and the people (Genesis 14:11-16).

And they plundered all the cities of Sodom and Gomorrah, and they also took Lot, Abram's brother's son, and his property, and they seized all the goods of the cities of Sodom, and they went away; and Unic, Abram's servant, who was in the battle, saw this, and told Abram all that the kings had done to the cities of Sodom, and that Lot was taken captive by them. And Abram heard this, and he rose up with about three hundred and eighteen men that were with him, and he that night pursued these kings and smote them, and they all fell before Abram and his men, and there was none remaining but the four kings who fled, and they went each his own road. And Abram recovered all the property of Sodom, and he also recovered Lot and his property, his wives and little ones and all belonging to him, so that Lot lacked nothing (Jasher 16:6-8).

Marriage of Abram to Hagar   35   1719 B.C.

Now Sarai, Abram's wife, bore him no children. She had an Egyptian maid whose name was Hagar; and Sarai said to Abram, "Behold now, the Lord has prevented me from bearing children; go in to my maid; it may be that I shall obtain children by her." And Abram hearkened to the voice of Sarai. So, after Abram had dwelt ten years in the land of

Canaan, Sarai, Abram's wife, took Hagar the Egyptian, her maid, and gave her to Abram her husband as a wife. And he went in to Hagar, and she conceived; and when she saw that she had conceived, she looked with contempt on her mistress (Genesis 16:1-4).

And Sarai the daughter of Haran, Abram's wife, was still barren in those days, she did not bear to Abram either son or daughter. And when she saw that she bare no children she took her handmaid Hagar, whom Pharaoh had given her, and she gave her to Abram her husband for a wife. . . . And Sarai said to Abram, "behold here is my handmaid Hagar, go to her that she may bring forth upon my knees, that I may also obtain children through her." And at the end of ten years of Abram's dwelling in the land of Canaan, which is the eighty fifth [35?] year of Abram's life, Sarai gave Hagar unto him. And Abram hearkened to the voice of his wife Sarai, and he took his handmaid Hagar and Abram came to her and she conceived (Jasher 16:23-24, 26-28).

Birth of Ishmael   36   1718 B.C.

And the angel of the Lord said to her [Hagar], "Behold, you are with child, and shall bear a son; you shall call his name Ishmael; because the Lord has given heed to your affliction." . . . And Hagar bore Abram a son; and Abram called the name of his son, whom Hagar bore, Ishmael. Abram was eighty-six [36?] years old when Hagar bore Ishmael to Abram (Genesis 16:11, 15-16).

And Hagar at that time returned to her master's house, and at the end of days Hagar bare a son to Abram, and Abram called his name Ishmael; and Abram was eighty-six [36?] years old when he begat him (Jasher 16:36).

2. From Terah to Thera

Change of names   49   1705 B.C.

When Abram was ninety-nine [49?] years old the Lord appeared to Abram, and said to him, "I am God Almighty; walk before me, and be blameless. And I will make my covenant between me and you, and will multiply you exceedingly.". . . "No longer shall your name be Abram, but your name shall be Abraham; for I have made you the father of a multitude of nations". . . . And God said to Abraham, "As for Sarai your wife, you shall not call her name Sarai, but Sarah shall be her name. I will bless her, and moreover I will give you a son by her; I will bless her, and she shall be a mother of nations; kings of peoples shall come from her" (Genesis 17:1-2, 5, 15-16).

And Abram the son of Terah was then ninety-nine [49?] years old. . . . And now therefore thy name shall no more be called Abram but Abraham, and thy wife shall no more be called Sarai but Sarah. For I will bless you both, and I will multiply your seed after you that you shall become a great nation, and kings shall come forth from you (Jasher 17:16, 19-20).

Destruction of Sodom   49   1705 B.C.

Then the Lord rained on Sodom and Gomorrah brimstone and fire from the Lord out of heaven; and he overthrew those cities, and all the valley, and all the inhabitants of the cities, and what grew on the ground. But Lot's wife behind him looked back, and she became a pillar of salt. And Abraham went early in the morning to the place where he had stood before the Lord; and he looked down toward Sodom and Gomorrah and toward all the land of the valley, and beheld, and lo, the smoke of the land went up like the smoke of a furnace (Genesis 19:24-28).

Then the Lord rained upon Sodom and upon Gomorrah and upon all these cities brimstone and fire from the Lord

Abram and His Times

out of heaven. And he overthrew these cities, all the plain and all the inhabitants of the cities, and that which grew upon the ground; and Ado the wife of Lot looked back to see the destruction of the cities, for her compassion was moved on account of her daughters who remained in Sodom, for they did not go with her. And when she looked back she became a pillar of salt, and it is yet in that place unto this day. . . . And Abraham rose up early in the morning to see what had been done to the cities of Sodom; and he looked and beheld the smoke of the cities going up like the smoke of a furnace (Jasher 19:51-53, 56).

Birth of Isaac   50   1704 B.C.

The Lord visited Sarah as he had said, and the Lord did to Sarah as he had promised. And Sarah conceived, and bore Abraham a son in his old age at the time of which God had spoken to him. Abraham called the name of his son who was born to him, whom Sarah bore him, Isaac. . . . Abraham was a hundred [50?] years old when his son Isaac was born to him (Genesis 21:1-3, 5).

And it was at that time at the end of a year and four months of Abraham's dwelling in the land of the Philistines in Gerar, that God visited Sarah, and the Lord remembered her, and she conceived and bare a son to Abraham. And Abraham called the name of the son which was born to him, which Sarah bare to him, Isaac. . . . [A]nd Abraham was one hundred [50?], and Sarah ninety [40?] years old, when Isaac was born to them (Jasher 21:1-2, 3).

Death of Sarah   67   1687 B.C.

Sarah lived a hundred and twenty-seven [57?] years; these were the years of the life of Sarah. And Sarah died at Kiriath-arba (that is, Hebron) in the land of Canaan; and Abraham went in to mourn for Sarah and to weep for her (Genesis 23:1-2).

2. From Terah to Thera

And the life of Sarah was one hundred and twenty seven [57?] years, and Sarah died; and Abraham rose up from before his dead to seek a burial place to bury his wife Sarah; and he went and spoke to the children of Heth, the inhabitants of the land. . . . And the days of Sarah were one hundred and twenty seven [57?] years and she died, and Abraham made a great and heavy mourning, and he performed the rites of mourning for seven days (Jasher 24:1, 15).

Isaac marries Rebekah   70   1684 B.C.

Then Isaac brought her into the tent, and took Rebekah, and she became his wife; and he loved her. So Isaac was comforted after his mother's death. . . . These are the descendants of Isaac, Abraham's son: Abraham was the father of Isaac, and Isaac was forty [20?] years old when he took to wife Rebekah, the daughter of Bethuel. . . . (Genesis 24:67; 25:19-20).

And they all blessed the Lord who brought this thing about, and they gave him Rebecca, the daughter of Bethuel, for a wife for Isaac. . . . And Isaac took Rebecca and she became his wife, and he brought her into the tent. And Isaac was forty [20?] years old when he took Rebecca, the daughter of his uncle Bethuel, for a wife (Jasher 24:39, 44-45).

Abraham marries Keturah   70   1684 B.C.

Abraham took another wife whose name was Keturah. She bore him Zimran, Jokshan, Medan, Midian, Ishbak, and Shuah" (Genesis 25:1-2).

And it was at that time that Abraham again took a wife in his old age, and her name was Keturah, from the land of Canaan. And she bare unto him Zimrau, Yokshan, Medan, Midian, Yishbak and Shuach, being six sons (Jasher 25:1-2).

Abram and His Times

Rebekah has twins, Esau and Jacob   71   1683 B.C.

And Isaac prayed to the Lord for his wife, because she was barren; and the Lord granted his prayer, and Rebekah his wife conceived. . . . When her days to be delivered were fulfilled, behold, there were twins in her womb (Genesis 25:21, 24).

And the Lord heard the prayer of Isaac the son of Abraham, and the Lord was intreated of him and Rebecca his wife conceived. . . . And when her [Rebecca's] days to be delivered were completed, she knelt down, and behold there were twins in her womb, as the Lord had spoken to her (Jasher 26:8, 13).

Death of Abraham   75   1679 B.C.

These are the days of the years of Abraham's life, a hundred and seventy-five [75?] years. Abraham breathed his last and died in a good old age, an old man and full of years, and was gathered to his people (Genesis 25:7-8).

[A]nd all the days of Abraham were one hundred and seventy-five [75?] years, and he died and was gathered to his people in good old age, old and satisfied with days, and Isaac and Ishmael his sons buried him (Jasher 26:29).

Birth of Joseph   1664 B.C.

[This birth date of Joseph was inferred previously from Egyptian records.[5]]

Famine in the land (Isaac's famine)   1654 B.C.

Now there was a famine in the land, besides the former famine that was in the days of Abraham. And Isaac went to Gerar, to Abimelech king of the Philistines. And the Lord appeared to him, and said, "Do not go down to Egypt; dwell in the land of which I shall tell you. Sojourn in this land, and I will be with you, and will bless you; for to you and to your descendants I will give all these lands, and I will fulfil the oath which I swore to Abraham your father" (Genesis 26:1-3).

And in those days, after the death of Abraham, in that year the Lord brought a heavy famine in the land, and whilst the famine was raging in the land of Canaan, Isaac rose up to go down to Egypt on account of the famine, as his father Abraham had done. And the Lord appeared that night to Isaac and he said to him, do not go down to Egypt but rise and go to Gerar, to Abimelech king of the Philistines, and remain there till the famine shall cease. And Isaac rose up and went to Gerar, as the Lord commanded him, and he remained there a full year (Jasher 28:1-3).

Famine in the land (Jacob's famine)   **1628 B.C.**

[One of the most dramatic climate events in recorded history was that associated with the eruption of the Thera volcano near Crete in the Mediterranean Sea. That eruption occurred in about 1628 B.C., and it caused major climate disruptions in the biblically important areas of Egypt and Canaan lasting for several years.[6]]

3. WICKEDNESS OF SODOM

As a starting point for this subject, it is helpful to consider the origin and some of the geographical aspects of the famously wicked cities of the plain. The origin of these cities is said to have been the following:

> And four men from the family of Ham [son of Noah] went to the land of the plain; these are the names of the four men, Sodom, Gomorrah, Admah, and Zeboyim.
> And these men built themselves four cities in the land of the plain, and they called the names of their cities after their own names.
> And they and their children and all belonging to them dwelt in those cities, and they were fruitful and multiplied greatly and dwelt peaceably (Jasher 10:25-27).

In a later independent development another important city was established.

> And some of the children of Shem son of Noah . . . also went and built themselves cities in the places wherein they were scattered, and they called their cities after their names (Jasher 10:30).

> And in the second year after the tower [of Babel] a man from the house of Ashur [a son of Shem], whose

> name was Bela, went from the land of Ninevah to sojourn with his household wherever he could find a place; and they came until opposite the cities of the plain against Sodom, and they dwelt there.
>
> And the man rose up and built there a small city, and called its name Bela after his name; that is [in] the land of Zoar unto this day (Jasher 10:35-36).

Thus, Zoar was near the cities of the plain, but Bela's founder was a descendant of Shem rather than Ham.

At a later time the inhabitants of Zoar were also closely associated with Egypt.

> And upon the third day of his birth Pharaoh made a feast for his officers and servants, for the hosts of the land of Zoar and of the land of Egypt (Jasher 46:16).

> And all the wise men of the land of Egypt came before the king, together with all the magicians and sorcerers that were in Egypt and in Goshen, in Raamses, in Tachpanches, in Zoar, and in all the places on the borders of Egypt, and they all stood before the king (Jasher 48:14).

Further information regarding Zoar in different historical epochs was obtained through the descriptions of Arabian geographers, suggesting that Zoar served as an important station in the Aqaba-to-Jericho trade route, and through Eusebius' statement that the Dead Sea was situated between Zoar and Jericho. Researchers who have studied ancient texts portray Zoar as a town erected in the middle of a flourishing oasis, watered by rivers flowing down from the high Moab Mountains in the east. . . . An adjacent cave is ascribed as the location where Lot and his daughters took refuge during the destruction of Sodom.[7]

3. Wickedness of Sodom

Unfortunately, Abram's nephew Lot preferred to live in the city of Sodom.

> And Lot lifted up his eyes, and saw that the Jordan valley was well watered everywhere like the garden of the Lord [Garden of Eden], like the land of Egypt, in the direction of Zoar; this was before the Lord destroyed Sodom and Gomorrah. So Lot chose for himself all the Jordan valley, and Lot journeyed east; thus they [Abram and Lot] separated from each other. Abram dwelt in the land of Canaan, while Lot dwelt among the cities of the valley and moved his tent as far as Sodom. Now the men of Sodom were wicked, great sinners against the Lord (Genesis 13:10-13).

The sites of Sodom, Gomorrah, Zoar, and most of the other places mentioned here are known today.

> Then the Lord said, "Because the outcry against Sodom and Gomorrah is great and their sin is very grave, I will go down to see whether they have done altogether according to the outcry which has come to me; and if not, I will know" (Genesis 18:20-21).

> But before they [two angels] lay down, the men of the city, the men of Sodom, both young and old, all the people to the last man, surrounded the house; and they called to Lot "Where are the men [Lot's holy guests] who came to you tonight? Bring them out to us, that we may know them." Lot went out of the door to the men, shut the door after him, and said, "I beg you, my brothers, do not act so wickedly. Behold, I have two daughters who have not known man; let me bring them out to you, and do to them as you please; only do nothing to these men, for they have come under the shelter of my roof." But they said, "Stand Back!" And they said, "This fellow [Lot] came to sojourn,

and he would play the judge! Now we will deal worse with you [Lot] than with them [the angels]." Then they pressed hard against the man Lot, and drew near to break the door. But the men [angels] put forth their hands and brought Lot into the house to them, and shut the door. And they struck with blindness the men who were at the door of the house [all the people], both small and great, so that they wearied themselves groping for the door (Genesis 19:4-11).

When morning dawned, the angels urged Lot, saying, "Arise, take your wife and your two daughters who are here, lest you be consumed in the punishment of the city." But he lingered; so the men seized him and his wife and his two daughters by the hand, the Lord being merciful to him, and they brought him forth and set him outside the city. And when they had brought them forth, they said, "Flee for your life; do not look back or stop anywhere in the valley; flee to the hills, lest you be consumed." And Lot said to them, "Oh, no, my lords; behold, your servant has found favor in your sight, and you have shown me great kindness in saving my life; but I cannot flee to the hills, lest the disaster overtake me, and I die. Behold, yonder city is near enough to flee to, and it is a little one. Let me escape there – is it not a little one? – and my life will be saved!" He [an angel] said to him [Lot], "Behold, I grant you this favor also, that I will not overthrow the city of which you have spoken. Make haste, escape there; for I can do nothing till you arrive there." Therefore the name of the city was called Zoar [that is little]. The sun had risen on the earth when Lot came to Zoar.

Then the Lord rained on Sodom and Gomorrah brimstone and fire from the Lord out of heaven; and he overthrew those cities, and all the valley, and all the inhabitants of the cities, and what grew on the ground. But Lot's wife behind him looked back, and she became a pillar of salt. And Abraham went early in the morning to the place where he had stood before the Lord; and he looked down toward Sodom and Gomorrah and toward all the land of the valley, and beheld, and lo, the smoke of the land went up like the smoke of a furnace (Genesis 19:15-28).

Now Lot went up out of Zoar, and dwelt in the hills with his two daughters, for he was afraid to dwell in Zoar; so he dwelt in a cave with his two daughters (Genesis 19:30).

The idea, mentioned above, of Lot's wife looking longingly back toward her home and consequently being converted into a pillar of salt has served as a subject for artists. The example shown below is located in the Franklin D. Murphy Sculpture Garden at UCLA.

Figure 2. Sculpture entitled "Lot's Wife," created by Anna Mahler, 1904-1988[8]

Pillars of salt are not uncommon near the Dead Sea, and one such pillar may have been interpreted by later visitors to that site as representing the deceased wife of Lot. While the original name "Lot's Wife" for the sculpture seems very reasonable, the sculpture garden later changed the title of the work to "Night," which has no obvious relationship to a white (salt-colored) statue of a woman looking longingly back toward her home and doomed relatives. "The change was requested by the artist in 1978 for the plaque and confirmed by her in 1983 for the catalogue published in 1984."[9]

The other concept mentioned above is that of Lot moving with his two daughters to a cave in the hills beyond Zoar. As it happens, the locations of Zoar and of Lot's Cave are both now well known. Concerning the cave, the following has been said.

> Beyond its amazing construction on the sheer mountain cliff, and its amazing view of the southern Dead Sea valley, the most intriguing aspect of the complex was the cave entered from the northern apse. While the entrance of the cave was paved with mosaics, most of it was left in its natural state. Beyond broken pieces of Byzantine pottery, archaeologists found pottery from as far back as the Early Bronze Age – the period of Abraham and Lot. This suggests the cave, high up in the mountain cliff, was occupied during that period. The monastery is situated about 7 km (4 mi) from Safi, the site identified on the Madaba Map as Zoar, the city God spared in the destruction (Genesis 19:20-23).
>
> Thus, in the region of Sodom and Gomorrah, a cave inhabited during the general period of Abraham and Lot was identified by the Byzantines as the cave Lot and his daughters stayed in after the destruction of Sodom and the Cities of the Plain (Genesis 19:30-38).[10]

The wickedness of the inhabitants of the cities of the valley (Sodom, Gomorrah, etc.) is clearly indicated in the biblical account as quoted above, but other examples of such wickedness are included in Jasher's treatment. Thus, four times per year the residents of the cities scheduled occasions of community sexual immorality.

> In those days all the people of Sodom and Gomorrah, and of the whole five cities, were exceedingly wicked and sinful against the Lord, and they provoked the Lord with their abominations, and they strengthened in acting abominably and scornfully before the Lord, and their wickedness and crimes were in those days great before the Lord.
> And they had in their land a very extensive valley, about half a day's walk, and in it there were fountains of water and a great deal of herbage surrounding the water.
> And all the people of Sodom and Gomorrah went there four times in the year, with their wives and children and all belonging to them, and they rejoiced there with timbrels and dances.
> And in the time of rejoicing they would all rise and lay hold of their neighbors' wives, and some, the virgin daughters of their neighbors, and they enjoyed them, and each man saw his wife and daughter in the hands of his neighbor and did not say a word.
> And they did so from morning to night, and they afterward returned home each man to his house and each woman to her tent; so they always did four times in the year (Jasher 18:11-15).

Besides such instances of sexual immorality, visitors to the cities were regularly robbed of their possessions and driven away impoverished.

> Also when a stranger came into their cities and brought goods which he had purchased with a view to dispose of there, the people of these cities would assemble, men, women and children, young and old, and

3. Wickedness of Sodom

go to the man and take his goods by force, giving a little to each man until there was an end to all the goods of the owner which he had brought into the land (Jasher 18:16).

Other visitors were tortured to death for the amusement of residents.

> And by desire of their four judges the people of Sodom and Gomorrah had beds erected in the streets of the cities, and if a man came to these places they laid hold of him and brought him to one of their beds, and by force made him to lie in them.
> And as he lay down, three men would stand at his head and three at his feet, and measure him by the length of the bed, and if the man was less than the bed these six men would stretch him at each end, and when he cried out to them they would not answer him.
> And if he was longer than the bed then they would draw together the two sides of the bed at each end, until the man had reached the gates of death (Jasher 19:3-5).

If a poor man came within the cities, he would be robbed of his clothes and denied food until he starved to death.

> And when a poor man came to their land they would give him silver and gold, and cause a proclamation in the whole city not to give him a morsel of bread to eat, and if the stranger should remain there some days, and die from hunger, not having been able to obtain a morsel of bread, then at his death all the people of the city would come and take their silver and gold which they had given to him.
> [A]t his death they also stripped him of his garments, and they would fight about them, and he that prevailed over his neighbor took them (Jasher 19:8-9).

Abram and His Times

If a resident of the cities was found secretly to have been providing food to a stranger, the resident would be executed. A very kind daughter of Lot named Paltith was a victim of this dreadful policy. Paltith's punishment was the following.

> And the people of Sodom and Gomorrah assembled and kindled a fire in the street of the city, and they took the woman [Paltith] and cast her into the fire and she was burned to ashes (Jasher 19:35).

Another instance of such an execution is included here.

> And in the city of Admah there was a woman to whom they did the like. . . . And he [a traveler] asked her for a drink of water. . . . And the young woman went into the house and fetched the man bread and water to eat and drink. And this affair became known to the people of Admah. . . . And the people of those cities assembled and brought out the young woman, and anointed her with honey from head to foot, ...and they placed her before a swarm of bees which were then in their hives, and the bees flew upon her and stung her that her whole body was swelled. And the young woman cried out on account of the bees, but no one took notice of her or pitied her, and her cries ascended to heaven. And the Lord was provoked at this and at all the works of the cities of Sodom, for they had abundance of food and had tranquility amongst them, and still would not sustain the poor and the needy (Jasher 19:36-44).

As illustrated in these and other incidents, it should never be forgotten that the Lord has great sympathy for the poor and the needy, while on the other hand he has disdain for the rich and the greedy.

3. Wickedness of Sodom

Wickedness as indicated above was, of course, not restricted to the cities of the plain or to the time of Lot. Thus, other occurrences of sexual immorality were also associated with ancestors of the Israelites including in an earlier era those in the vicinity of the Garden of Eden.

> They began to go down from the Holy Mountain one after another, and to mix with the children of Cain, in foul fellowships.[11]
>
> And when they looked at the daughters of Cain, at their beautiful figures, and at their hands and feet dyed with colour, and tattooed in ornaments on their faces, the fire of sin was kindled in them. . . , until they committed abomination with them.[12]
>
> And God was angry with them, and repented of them because they had come down from glory, and had thereby lost or forsaken their own purity or innocence, and were fallen into the defilement of sin.[13]

Similar transgressions occurred at the base of Mt. Sinai after the exodus from Egypt. That this was also considered to be a holy mountain or mountain of God may be seen, for example, in the following verses: Exodus 3:1; 4:27; 18:5; 19:3, 17; 24:13; 31:18; Deuteronomy 9:10; 1 Kings 19:8. The golden calf episode in the Bible at the base of this holy mountain includes the following report:

> When Moses didn't come back down the mountain right away, the people went to Aaron. "Look," they said, "make us a god to lead us, for this fellow Moses who brought us here from Egypt has disappeared; something must have happened to him." "Give me your gold earrings," Aaron replied. So they all did – men and women, boys and girls. Aaron melted the gold then

molded and tooled it into the form of a calf. The people exclaimed, "O Israel, this is the god that brought you out of Egypt!" When Aaron saw how happy the people were about it, he built an altar before the calf and announced, "Tomorrow there will be a feast to Jehovah!" So they were up early the next morning and began offering burnt offerings and peace offerings to the calf idol; afterwards they sat down to feast and drink at a wild party, followed by sexual immorality.

Then the Lord told Moses "Quick! Go on down, for your people that you brought from Egypt have defiled themselves, and have quickly abandoned all my laws. They have molded themselves a calf, and worshiped it, and sacrificed to it, and said, "This is your god, O Israel, that brought you out of Egypt" (Exodus 32:1-8 TLB).

When they came near the camp, Moses saw the calf and the dancing, and in terrible anger he threw the tablets to the ground, and they lay broken at the foot of the mountain. He took the calf and melted it in the fire, and when the metal cooled, he ground it into powder and spread it upon the water and made the people drink it. Then he turned to Aaron. "What in the world did the people do to you," he demanded, "to make you bring such a terrible sin upon them?" "Don't get so upset," Aaron replied. "You know these people and what a wicked bunch they are. They said to me, 'Make us a god to lead us, for something has happened to this fellow Moses who led us out of Egypt.' Well, I told them, 'Bring me your gold earrings.' So they brought them to me and I threw them into the fire, and . . . well . . . this calf came out!" When Moses saw that the people had been committing adultery – at Aaron's encouragement, and much to the amusement of their enemies – he stood at the camp entrance and shouted, "All of you who are on the Lord's side, come over here and join me." And all the Levites came. He told them, "Jehovah the God of Israel says 'Get your swords and go back and forth from one end of the camp to the other and kill even your brothers, friends, and neighbors.' " So they did, and about three thousand men died that day (Exodus 32:19-28 TLB).

Thus, in both the Eden and Sinai stories, the people of God are said to have engaged in sexual immorality near a holy mountain. Similar conduct may also have occurred during the reign of King Josiah at the Temple Mount in Jerusalem.

> He also tore down the houses of male prostitution around the Temple, where the women wove robes for the Asherah idol (2 Kings 23:7 TLB).

The Bible includes several other statements that explicitly forbid a variety of sins. Further examples from the Old Testament include the following.

> Adultery: "You shall not commit adultery" (Exodus 20:14 RSV).

> Lust: "You shall not covet your neighbor's house; you shall not covet your neighbor's wife, or his manservant, or his maidservant, or his ox, or his ass, or anything that is your neighbor's" (Exodus 20:17).

> Beastiality: "Whoever lies with a beast shall be put to death" (Exodus 22:19).

> Homosexuality: "You shall not lie with a male as with a woman; it is an abomination" (Leviticus 18:22). "If a man lies with a male as with a woman, both of them have committed an abomination; they shall be put to death" (Leviticus 20:13).

Statements concerning sin and punishment also occur in the New Testament including those of Jesus.

> Think not that I have come to abolish the law and the prophets; I have come not to abolish them but to fulfil them. For truly, I say to you, till heaven and earth pass away, not an iota, not a dot, will pass from the law until all is accomplished. Whoever then relaxes one of the least of these commandments and teaches men so, shall be called least in the kingdom of heaven; but he who does them and teaches them shall be called great in the kingdom of heaven. For I tell you, unless your righteousness exceeds that of the scribes and Pharisees, you will never enter the kingdom of heaven (Matthew 5:17-20).

> At that time the disciples came to Jesus, saying, "Who is the greatest in the kingdom of heaven?" And calling to him a child, he put him in the midst of them, and said, "Truly, I say to you, unless you turn and become like children, you will never enter the kingdom of heaven. Whoever humbles himself like this child, he is the greatest in the kingdom of heaven."
> "Whoever receives one such child in my name receives me; but whoever causes one of these little ones who believe in me to sin, it would be better for him to have a great millstone fastened round his neck and to be drowned in the depth of the sea."
> "Woe to the world for temptations to sin! For it is necessary that temptations come, but woe to the man by whom the temptation comes!" (Matthew 18:1-7).

Similar sentiments were expressed by Paul and others.

> God gave them up to dishonorable passions. Their women exchanged natural relations for unnatural, and the

men likewise gave up natural relations with women and were consumed with passion for one another, men committing shameless acts with men and receiving in their own persons the due penalty for their error.

And since they did not see fit to acknowledge God, God gave them up to a base mind and to improper conduct. They were filled with all manner of wickedness, evil, covetousness, malice. Full of envy, murder, strife, deceit, malignity, they are gossips, slanderers, haters of God, insolent, haughty, boastful, inventors of evil, disobedient to parents, foolish, faithless, heartless, ruthless. Though they know God's decree that those who do such things deserve to die, they not only do them but approve those who practice them (Romans 1:26-32).

Do you not know that the unrighteous will not inherit the kingdom of God. Do not be deceived; neither the immoral, nor idolaters, nor adulterers, nor homosexuals, nor thieves, nor the greedy, nor drunkards, nor revilers, nor robbers will inherit the kingdom of God (1 Corinthians 6:9-10).

For this is the will of God, your sanctification: that you abstain from immorality; that each one of you know how to take a wife for himself in holiness and honor, not in the passion of lust like heathen who do not know God; that no man transgress, and wrong his brother in this matter, because the Lord is an avenger in all these things, as we solemnly forewarned you. For God has not called us for uncleanness, but in holiness. Therefore whoever disregards this, disregards not man but God, who gives his Holy Spirit to you. (1 Thessalonians 4:3-8).

But I have a few things against you: you have some there who hold the teaching of Balaam, who taught Balak to put a stumbling block before the sons of Israel, that they might eat food sacrificed to idols and practice immorality. (Revelation 2:14).

It should be clear from the preceding paragraphs of this section that there are several Bible-related stories, admonitions, and warnings on the subject of sexual and other sins and their consequences. In the Old Testament period this content is associated with the Garden of Eden, the exodus, Sodom, and the Israelite temple. Strict injunctions against such sinful behavior are also given throughout the New Testament era. In view of the biblical condemnation of such practices, it is striking that they continue today with substantial popularity among individuals who consider themselves to be Christians, and they are even approved by some church denominations. If biblical teachings are to be taken seriously, it would seem that many people who anticipate salvation may be tragically disappointed.

4. DESTRUCTION OF SODOM AND GOMORRAH

The preceding section has emphasized the wickedness of the inhabitants of the cities of the plain, as well as the antibiblical sins of other people throughout history. Given this wickedness, it is not surprising that severe punishment would often be the result. The first phase of the punishment in Sodom was the blinding of the residents. Lot and his family had taken refuge in his house with the assistance of two angels. All other residents of Sodom surrounded the house and sought to break down the door. Before they could do that, however, they were all blinded so that they could not even locate the door of Lot's house. This circumstance permitted Lot and his (willing) family members to escape. The most natural cause of such widespread blindness would seem to have been an intense flash of light. The people inside of Lot's house, on the other hand, would have been protected from any such flash because, as Lot said, they were "under the shelter of my roof" (Genesis 19:8).

It can be suggested that a blinding flash of light might have been a consequence of an asteroid impact. The incidence of the Tunguska asteroid in Siberia in 1908 may provide an analogy. The light and heat from that event were responsible for the starting of major fires, and several eyewitness accounts may be of interest.

> At that moment I became so hot that I couldn't bear it as if my shirt was on fire. . . . Then I saw a wonder: trees were falling, the branches were on fire, it became mighty bright, how can I say this, as if there was a second sun, my eyes were hurting, I even closed them. . . . [T]he peasants saw to the northwest, rather high above the horizon, some strangely bright (impossible to look at) bluish-white heavenly body, which for 10 minutes moved downwards. . . . All villagers were stricken with panic and took to the streets, women cried, thinking it was the end of the world."[14]

In comparison to the Tunguska event, the sequence of occurrences leading up to the destruction of Sodom seems to have been more complicated. There is still disagreement on this subject and the following sentences represent a possible synthesis. It seems that the first step in the destruction process may have been the impact of an asteroid above the north end of the Dead Sea. It has been claimed that such an impact occurred in about 1700 B.C.[15] This date is in good agreement with the date of about 1705 B.C. inferred in Section 2 above for the "Destruction of Sodom." East of the sea the impact flattened all of the buildings in the northeast direction down to their stone foundations. Chemical analysis has shown that the destruction area was then inundated by a wash of salt water in the northeasterly direction from the Dead Sea. The impact also brought short-duration but extremely high temperatures which melted the surfaces of rocks and pottery sherds in the impact area.

4. Destruction of Sodom and Gomorrah

As just mentioned, the asteroid impact seemingly occurred above the north end of the Dead Sea. On the other hand, the Valley of Siddim and the cities of the plain are generally understood to have been located in the well-watered area south of the Dead Sea. By analogy with records of the Tunguska event, the impact over the Dead Sea can reasonably be associated with the intense flash of light that blinded Lot's adversaries in Sodom. There remains, however, the question of the subsequent fire and brimstone that is said to have destroyed the cities of the plain.

As mentioned in Section 3, following the blinding of the residents of Sodom, Lot was urged to take his family and flee east into the hills.

> Then the Lord rained on Sodom and Gomorrah brimstone and fire from the Lord out of heaven; and he overthrew those cities, and all the valley, and all the inhabitants of the cities, and what grew on the ground (Genesis 19:24-25).

> And Abraham went early in the morning to the place where he had stood before the Lord; and he looked down toward Sodom and Gomorrah and toward all the land of the valley, and beheld, and lo, the smoke of the land went up like the smoke of a furnace (Genesis 19:27-28).

In the above paragraphs it has been inferred that an incident asteroid may have caused the blinding of the residents of Sodom who were wandering outside in the vicinity of Lot's house. Now we find that the next morning, after Lot's escape to Zoar and the hills east of the valley, a further disaster befell the remaining residents of the valley.

Abram and His Times

> The sun had risen on the earth when Lot came to Zoar (Genesis 19:23).

Lot's plan to go up out of the small city of Zoar and hide in the hills seems to have been a good concept. A cave could be the most secure location in the occurrence of a storm of burning material, and the most likely place for caves to be found would have been in the hills above the valley floor. It was then that Sodom and Gomorrah and all other remaining residents of the valley were destroyed in a blaze of brimstone and fire.

The biblical account doesn't state explicitly what was burning in the plain to create the appearance of the smoke of a furnace. It may be noted, however, that common furnace fuels today include petroleum products such as oil and natural gas. Thus, it is not unreasonable to enquire whether any such fuels might have occurred naturally in the plain after the impact of an asteroid and its various consequences. This inquiry will be considered in the following paragraphs.

The asteroid impact seems likely to have occurred over the Dead Sea. On the other hand, the Valley of Siddim and the cities of the plain are generally understood to have been located in the well-watered area south of the Dead Sea. Nevertheless, the destruction of Sodom and the other cities of the plain may have been a secondary effect of the asteroid impact. Past commentators have suggested locations for the cities both to the north and south of the Dead Sea.

> The reference to "bitumen pits" in Genesis 14:10, however, tips the scale in favor of a southern location. Bitumen (a natural petroleum product similar to asphalt)

was commonly found in the shallow southern basin of the Dead Sea in antiquity.[16]

The Bible provides a detailed description of the calamity that befell the cities of the plain. In that description are two Hebrew phrases and a Hebrew word that must be examined in order to understand the event: *goprit wa es*, the material that fell on the cities (Genesis 19:24), *hapak*, what happened to the cities (Genesis 19:25), and *kqitor hakkibsan*, what Abraham observed (Genesis 19:28).

The word *goprit* is a foreign loan word, most likely derived from Akkadian *ki/ubritu*, which means sulfurous oil (black sulfur). The word accompanying *goprit*, *wa es*, simply means "and fire." In other words, the material that fell on Sodom and Gomorrah and the cities of the plain (except Zoar) was a burning petroleum product.[17]

When Abraham looked down upon the scene of devastation, he observed smoke rising from the land of the plain, *k^{e}qitor hakkibsan*, "like smoke from a furnace." ... The Biblical description, then, of the destruction was of burning material raining down from above, accompanied by an overturning of the cities and thick smoke being forced upward from the land.[18]

As noted above, bitumen and other petroleum products have long been found in the southern basin of the Dead Sea. Under normal conditions there is usually only a gradual and harmless seepage of these hydrocarbons to the surface from underground reservoirs. This seepage is slow and intermittent, tending to occur along existing fault lines. There are two relevant fault lines near the Dead Sea. These both have a north-south alignment. One of them is at the western edge of the sea, and the other is at the eastern edge.

A possible explanation for the destruction of the Cities of the Plain is that pressure from an earthquake caused underground flammable petroleum products to be forced up through the fault lines. They then became ignited and rained down on the surrounding countryside. The sites of Bab edh-Dhra [probably Sodom] and Numeira [probably Gomorrah] are located precisely on the eastern fault line.[19]

[T]he region south of the Dead Sea is very unstable, being bordered by fault lines on the east and west. Earthquakes are common in this area. After surveying the geology of the district, Clapp concluded that combustible materials from the earth destroyed the cities. He found bitumen and petroleum in the area. Natural gas and sulfur, which normally accompany bitumen and petroleum, are also present. These combustible materials could have been forced from the earth by subterranean pressure brought about by an earthquake resulting from the shifting of the bounding faults. Geologists who have studied the area in recent times agree with Clapp's reconstruction. If lightning or surface fires ignited these combustibles as they came spewing forth from the ground, it would indeed result in a holocaust such as described in Genesis 19. It is significant to note that both Bab edh-Dhra and Numeira lie at the edge of the plain, *exactly on the eastern fault line!*

Abraham's eyewitness description fits the theory of a conflagration of petroleum products, for such a conflagration would result in a thick black smoke being forced into the sky by the heat and pressure of the burning materials shooting out of the fissure in the earth.[20]

The earthquake caused either an uplift in the vicinity of the site [of Numeira] or a down-dropping of the rift valley to the west, resulting in a 50 m (164 ft) increase in elevation differential between the town site and Wadi Numeira to the north.[21]

4. Destruction of Sodom and Gomorrah

This relative vertical translation is believed to have facilitated the release of combustible materials from underground reservoirs.

In summary, the subject of the destruction of the cities of the plain is somewhat complicated, but the entire process was probably initiated by the impact of an asteroid. The first consequences of the impact are similar to, but seemingly more severe than, those reported for the Tunguska event of 1908. The Tunguska impact started fires in the trees and caused bright lights in the sky which forced observers to close their eyes or turn away. The Dead Sea asteroid event, on the other hand, flattened cities, melted the surfaces of rocks and pottery sherds, initiated large waves on the Dead Sea, and (according to the Bible) instantly blinded anyone exposed to its radiated light even at a considerable distance from the impact. This information taken together suggests that the Dead Sea asteroid impact may have been of greater magnitude than the Tunguska event.

The fires that destroyed the cities of the plain seem to have been caused by the ignition of petroleum products that were released during the approximately 50 meter vertical offset in the fault line along the eastern edge of the Valley of Siddim south of the Dead Sea. The blinding of residents of the cities of the plain, the fault-line slippage, the petroleum leakage, and the city-destroying fires were all consequences of the asteroid impact. On the other hand, the massive eruption of the Thera volcano, which lies along a Mediterranean fault, occurred several years later, as discussed in Section 6. That eruption may nevertheless have been a delayed consequence of the same asteroid impact.

A listing of relative tree-ring numbers, calendar years B.C., and normalized tree-ring thickness (in Anatolia) for the time period around the asteroid impact (over the Dead Sea) is included in Table 3. This table assumes the accuracy of the chronology of Section 2 above. Thus, the consequences of the impact include a diminished tree-ring thickness starting between about 1705 B.C. and 1704 B.C. and lasting for about three years. An approximate listing of the most important chronological period for this impact and its associated famine is included here in Table 3.

Table 3. Anatolian dendrochronology in relative tree-ring numbers, calendar years B.C., and normalized tree-ring thickness for the time period around a major growth anomaly associated with an asteroid impact near the Dead Sea during the lifetime of Abraham.

Tree-Ring Numbers	Calendar Years B.C.	Tree-Ring Thickness	Famine Years
772	1708	89.6	
773	1707	86.1	
774	1706	102.7	
775	**1705**	97.1	
776	1704	74.6	1
777	1703	72.4	2
778	1702	72.0	3
779	1701	96.4	
780	1700	103.4	
781	1699	116.4	
782	1698	120.4	
783	1697	86.3	

It would appear from the tree-ring thicknesses listed in this table that a substantial decrease in growth conditions occurred at some time between about 1705 and 1704 B.C. This reduced growth period lasted for about three years and may be associated with the release into the atmosphere of toxic fumes from the burning of petroleum products during the destruction of the cities of the plain. A graphical presentation of the tree-ring thickness chronology is shown in Figure 3.

The period of reduced growth is of longer duration than the corresponding reduced-growth period associated with volcanic eruptions as will be seen in Section 6 below. Also, the post-impact growth-rate recovery is less dramatic than the post-eruption growth rates associated with a volcanogenic fertilization effect.[22]

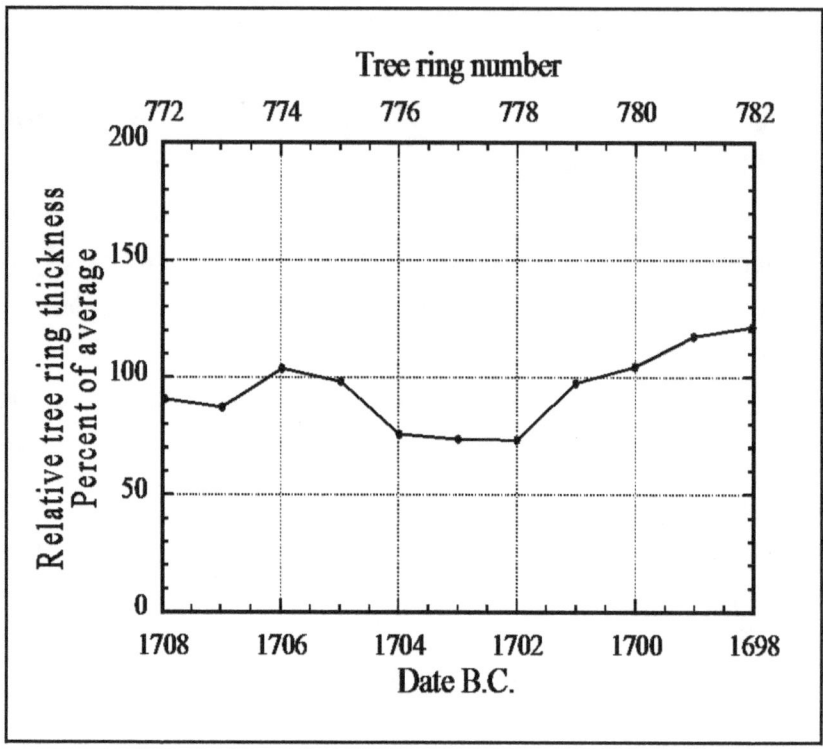

Figure 3. Relative tree-ring thickness for a growth anomaly in Anatolia that may be associated with an asteroid impact in the vicinity of the Dead Sea. The post-impact diminished growth period extended from at least 1704 B.C. to 1702 B.C.

5. SARAH HAS A BABY

As noted in Section 2 above, Sarai was born in about 1744 B.C., and by about 1732 B.C. Sarai was referred to as Abram's wife. However, by 1719 B.C. Sarai was about twenty-five years old, but she still had borne Abram no children. Without medical intervention, it is increasingly unusual for women today to have babies after they are about 40 years of age. This is entirely consistent with the story of Sarah becoming the mother of Isaac. To begin this story, it is helpful to consider a few quotations from the Bible.

> They [the visiting angels] said to him [Abraham], "Where is Sarah your wife?" And he said, "She is in the tent." The Lord said, "I will surely return to you in the spring, and Sarah your wife shall have a son." And Sarah was listening at the tent door behind him. Now Abraham and Sarah were old, advanced in age; it had ceased to be with Sarah after the manner of women. So Sarah laughed to herself, saying, "After I have grown old, and my husband is old, shall I have pleasure?" The Lord said to Abraham, "Why did Sarah laugh, and say, 'Shall I indeed bear a child, now that I am old?' Is anything too hard for the Lord? At the appointed time I will return to you, in the spring, and Sarah shall have a son." But Sarah denied,

saying "I did not laugh;" for she was afraid. He said, "No, but you did laugh" (Genesis 18:9-15).

The Lord visited Sarah as he had said, and the Lord did to Sarah as he had promised. And Sarah conceived, and bore Abraham a son in his old age at the time of which God had spoken to him. Abraham called the name of his son who was born to him, whom Sarah bore him, Isaac. And Abraham circumcised his son Isaac when he was eight days old, as God had commanded him. Abraham was a hundred [50?] years old when his son Isaac was born to him. And Sarah said "God has made laughter for me; every one who hears will laugh over me." And she said, "Who would have said to Abraham that Sarah would suckle children? Yet I have borne him a son in his old age" (Genesis 21:1-7).

The Genesis story of the birth of Isaac doesn't indicate the actual age of Sarah at the time of Isaac's birth, but that information can be obtained from other Bible-related sources such as Jubilees and Jasher.

And God said unto Abraham: "As for Sarai thy wife, her name will no more be called Sarai, but Sarah will be her name. And I shall bless her, and give thee a son by her, and I shall bless him, and he will become a nation, and kings of nations will proceed from him." And Abraham fell on his face, and rejoiced, and said in his heart: "Shall a son be born to him that is a hundred [50?] years old, and shall Sarah, who is ninety [40?] years old, bring forth?" And Abraham said unto God: "O that Ishmael might live before thee!" And God said: "Yea, and Sarah also will bear thee a son, and thou wilt call his name Isaac, and I shall establish My covenant with him, an everlasting covenant, and for his seed after him. And as for Ishmael also have I heard thee, and behold I shall

5. Sarah Has a Baby

bless him, and make him great, and multiply him exceedingly, and he will beget twelve princes, and I shall make him a great nation. But My covenant shall I establish with Isaac, whom Sarah will bear to thee, in these days, in the next year" (Jubilees 15:15-21).

And it was at that time at the end of a year and four months of Abraham's dwelling in the land of the Philistines in Gerar, that God visited Sarah, and the Lord remembered her, and she conceived and bare a son to Abraham. And Abraham called the name of the son which was born to him, which Sarah bare to him, Isaac. And Abraham circumcised his son Isaac at eight days old, as God had commanded Abraham to do unto his seed after him; and Abraham was one hundred [50?], and Sarah ninety [40?] years old, when Isaac was born to them (Jasher 21:1-3).

It is clear from the immediately preceding discussions regarding the birth of Isaac that non-biblical books such as Jasher and Jubilees might sometimes contain helpful information that is not included in the Bible. It could seem natural to be dismissive of such sources. On the other hand, the Bible states explicitly in two or three places that its contents are based on information from the Book of Jasher. Those instances include as a first example the following:

> Then spoke Joshua to the Lord in the day when the Lord gave the Amorites over to the men of Israel; and he said in the sight of Israel,
>
> "Sun, stand thou still at Gibeon, and thou Moon in the valley of Aijalon."
>
> And the sun stood still, and the moon stayed, until the nation took vengeance on their enemies.

Is this not written in the Book of Jashar? The sun stayed in the midst of heaven, and did not hasten to go down for about a whole day. There has been no day like it before or since, when the Lord hearkened to the voice of a man; for the Lord fought for Israel (Joshua 10:12-14).

The corresponding account from Jasher includes the following:

And the children of Israel pursued them [the Amorites], and they still smote them in the road, going on and smiting them.

And when they were smiting, the day was declining toward evening, and Joshua said in the sight of all the people, sun, stand thou still upon Gibeon, and thou moon in the valley of Ajalon, until the nation shall have revenged itself upon its enemies.

And the Lord hearkened to the voice of Joshua, and the sun stood still in the midst of the heavens, and it stood still six and thirty moments, and the moon also stood still and hastened not to go down a whole day.

And there was no day like that, before it or after it, that the Lord hearkened to the voice of a man, for the Lord fought for Israel (Jasher 88:62-65).

A second example is the following:

And David lamented with this lamentation over Saul and Jonathan his son, and he said it [the bow] should be taught to the people of Judah; behold, it is written in the Book of Jashar [or the upright]. He said:

"Thy glory, O Israel, is slain upon thy high places!

How are the mighty fallen!

Tell it not in Gath,

5. Sarah Has a Baby

publish it not in the streets of Ashkelon;
lest the daughters of the Philistines rejoice,
lest the daughters of the uncircumcised exult."
(2 Samuel 1:17-20).

This example seems not to be included in present copies of Jasher.

The above limited but explicit information suggests that statements provided by Jasher should not be too quickly discounted. It is for that reason that several references to Jasher have been included in the preceding discussions in this work. More specifically, dates and time periods provided by Jasher can possibly be of help in developing a chronology for the life of Abram and his family.

6. THREE ERUPTIONS OF THERA

It seems commonly to be understood that a volcanic eruption is an event involving a single volcano and occurring over a short period of time. The reality, however, may be somewhat different with several related eruptive events of a volcano occurring over a period of many years. This is the pattern observed with the eruptions of the Thera volcano in the second millennium B.C., including one of the largest volcanic events in history. An important source of information concerning the Thera eruptions is the book of Genesis in the Bible.

A detailed study of the Thera eruption sequence was carried out by Platon.[23] The ultimate Thera eruption is usually now dated to about 1628 B.C., but it is said to have been preceded by smaller eruptions that occurred earlier by several years. One approximate means for dating eruptions of Thera has employed core samples of sediment from the bottom of the sea near the island. These samples show clearly the presence of multiple layers of volcanic ash separated in their time of deposition by a few decades. The subtitle "Dating the Eruption[24] and an excerpt from a section on this subject by Platon are included here.

Dating the Eruption

More accurate examination of the layer of upper ash on one of the cores, however, has confirmed that the eruption occurred in three successive stages, since three alternating layers of coarse or finer ash have been distinguished. This means that the volcano continued to be active for a long time and that it had three successive eruptions separated by some years. The second one caused the destruction of the settlements and the consequent devastation of the island, but the last was the one which caused the submersion of a portion of it. The three layers of ash were also distinguished on Thera.[25]

It is striking that the three eruptions of Thera have a close parallel in the three periods of famine reported in Genesis. If one could determine the dates of the eruptions, then one could perhaps also establish the dates of the famine incidents reported in the Bible. The last and largest eruption of Thera is the most easily recognized biblical eruption event. The magnitude of this eruption and its consequences in somewhat distant Anatolia have been noted previously.

> An oddity at Porsuk [in Anatolia] is an enormous spike in growth at ca. 1650 B.C. The spike occurs in 61 out of 61 junipers, cedars, and pines, ranging in age from 19 to 244 years, and reflects a spring/summer growing season that was extraordinarily cool and moist. This is the most remarkable such anomaly in the last 9000 years, and we think it is a reaction to the eruption of Thera/Santorini some 820 kms to the west. The spikes taper off a year or two or three later, and the trees resume their normal lives until they are cut down.[26]

6. Three Eruptions of Thera

The date of this eruption is now usually considered to be about 1628 B.C., and this date is understood to mark the onset of a multiyear famine in Canaan and Egypt. The onset has also been indicated above in Section 2 of this text. An approximate listing of the most important chronological period for this eruption and its associated famine is included here in Table 4. A plot of the tree-ring variations for this eruption has been given previously.[27]

Table 4. Anatolian dendrochronology in relative tree-ring numbers, calendar years B.C., and normalized tree-ring thickness for the time period around a major growth anomaly during the lifetime of Jacob.

Tree-Ring Numbers	Calendar Years B.C.	Tree-Ring Thickness	Famine Years
850	1630	101.6	
851	1629	83.8	
852	**1628**	56.8	1
853	1627	52.4	2
854	1626	120.2	3
855	1625	165.6	4
856	1624	207.0	5
857	1623	184.2	6
858	1622	167.4	7
859	1621	155.0	
860	1620	124.3	

Abram and His Times

The immediately preceding and much smaller eruption of Thera occurred during the lifetime of Jacob's father Isaac in about 1654 B.C. as suggested in Section 2 above. An approximate listing of the most important chronological period for this eruption and its associated famine is included here in Table 5.

Table 5. Anatolian dendrochronology in relative tree-ring numbers, calendar years B.C., and normalized tree-ring thickness for the time period around a growth anomaly during the lifetime of Isaac.

Tree-Ring Numbers	Calendar Years B.C.	Tree-Ring Thickness	Famine Years
825	1655	95.5	
826	**1654**	65.2	1
827	1653	74.6	2
828	1652	92.0	3
829	1651	101.5	
830	1650	112.5	
831	1649	121.5	
832	1648	146.6	
833	1647	130.7	
834	1646	57.8	
835	1645	52.2	

The first Thera eruption of interest here occurred during the lifetime of Abram in about 1729 B.C. as indicated in Section 2.

6. Three Eruptions of Thera

An approximate listing of the most important chronological period for this eruption and its associated famine is included here in Table 6.

Table 6. Anatolian dendrochronology in relative tree-ring numbers, calendar years B.C., and normalized tree-ring thickness for the time period around a growth anomaly during the lifetime of Abram.

Tree-Ring Numbers	Calendar Years B.C.	Tree-Ring Thickness	Famine Years
750	1730	105.3	
751	**1729**	98.5	1
752	1728	123.0	2
753	1727	148.7	3
754	1726	146.1	
755	1725	104.5	
756	1724	106.3	
757	1723	130.1	
758	1722	109.4	
759	1721	119.3	
760	1720	105.9	

The three famine events documented in the Genesis record provide a close parallel with the sequence of three eruptions of the volcano on the island of Thera as noted by Platon and quoted earlier in this section. The last and most severe of the eruptions caused multi-year famine conditions at many locations in the northern hemisphere.

7. THE ASTEROID AND THE VOLCANO

Investigations of geophysical effects in the era near the lifetime of Abram and his family have revealed phenomena of two different types. As considered in connection with Table 6, there seems to have been a significant eruption of the Thera volcano in about 1729 B.C. This event occurred during the lifetime of Abram, and its consequence has been identified in Section 2 as "Abram's famine." That eruption altered the climate in Canaan, and the following famine caused Abram to travel with his family to Egypt, where they stayed until about 1722 B.C.

After the eruption events leading to "Abram's famine" as summarized above, the geophysical situation in the Middle East became more complicated because of the unanticipatable major impact of an asteroid in the vicinity of Sodom in about 1705 B.C.

> Then the Lord rained on Sodom and Gomorrah brimstone and fire from the Lord out of heaven; and he overthrew those cities, and all the valley, and all the inhabitants of the cities, and what grew on the ground (Genesis 19:24-25).

Abram and His Times

As is well known and was discussed here previously, this very dramatic and violent incident destroyed most human inhabitants from at least the southeast to the northeast sides of the Dead Sea.

What is perhaps not so well known is that this asteroid impact may also have affected the Minoan eruption behavior of the Thera volcano on the Greek island of Santorini. The Thera volcano is at about the center of the South Aegean Volcanic Arc, and other volcanic centers on this arc include Aegina, Methana, Poros, Milos, Kos, Yali, and Nysiros.[28] The asteroid impact that destroyed Sodom and other neighboring towns in about 1705 B.C. was located about 660 miles southeast from Thera. It may be recalled that a moderate eruption event had already occurred at Thera in 1729 B.C., before the asteroid impact. The violence of the nearby impact could have caused a dislocation on the volcanic arc leading to the further eruptions of Thera. The possibility that an asteroid impact could lead to a volcanic eruption has been considered previously.

> It has been suggested that large impacts can in some way trigger increased volcanism, or that there might be an even deeper connection.[29]

A somewhat similar eruption of the Thera volcano occurred in 1654 B.C., about seventy-five years after the first in 1729 B.C. This later eruption occurred during the lifetime of Jacob's father Isaac and has been identified in Section 2 above as "Isaac's famine." An approximate listing of the most important chronological period for this eruption and its associated famine is included in Table 5. That eruption also altered the climate in Canaan, and the following famine caused Isaac to consider

7. The Asteroid and the Volcano

traveling to Egypt as his father Abram had done. However, the Lord instructed Isaac not to go to Egypt but rather to live with the Philistines until the famine was over, so that is what he did (Genesis 26:1-5).

It has been suggested above that asteroid impacts might trigger volcanic eruptions. Thus, it seems possible that the impact of about 1705 B.C. might have been responsible, at least in part, for the massive eruption of Thera that occurred in about 1628 B.C. as represented in Table 4.

8. FREQUENCY OF ASTEROID IMPACTS

There are too many variables to make definitive statements about which asteroids might strike the surface of the earth, how much damage they might cause, and how often such incidents might occur. These variables would include at least such topics as the mass, speed, diameter, constitution, location, and direction of the asteroid. For present purposes this discussion will be simplified to include only the diameter, a commonly quoted parameter to represent the potential significance of an asteroid.

Asteroids smaller than roughly one meter in diameter are probably the most frequently seen category as they enter the earth's atmosphere where they burn up. Asteroids between about one meter and ten meters in diameter enter the earth's atmosphere at a frequency of roughly one every five years or so, and these asteroids are capable of causing substantial damage.[30] Thus, they may leave visible trails through the atmosphere, create craters, destroy buildings, flatten trees, start fires, and injure people and animals.

Asteroids in the size range of ten meters to one hundred meters are much less common, and data from many years in the past is mostly nonexistent. Perhaps one could estimate very roughly that the average rate of impacts by asteroids of this size would be about one per century. This estimated rate is based on only two events, namely the Chelyabinsk impact of 15 February 2013 (17-20 meter diameter) and the Tunguska event of 30 June 1908 (50 meter diameter). Similar impacts at earlier times must certainly have occurred, but for the most part any records of those events have by now been lost.

Fortunately, the asteroid impact that was responsible for the destruction of Sodom and neighboring cities in about 1705 B.C. is quite well documented in the Bible and related literature, and much information still exists. In addition, evidence of the heat of that impact can be seen in artifacts that recently have been recovered. This evidence is reminiscent of the destruction caused by the Tunguska event. The impact in North America by a larger ice-carrying comet or asteroid may have been responsible for Noah's flood in about 2035 B.C.[31] That incident may have caused an increase in mean sea level suggested to be as much as 350 to 450 feet,[32] and it seems to have brought about the extinction of the last mammoths on earth.[33]

Still larger impacts have occurred in the more distant past. Thus, many now extinct animals are believed to have perished in an impact event of about 12,900 years ago.

> Increasing evidence suggests that the extinction of many mammalian and avian taxa occurred abruptly and perhaps catastrophically at the onset of the Younger Dryas (YD), and this extinction was pronounced in North America where at least 35 mammal genera disappeared, including mammoths, mastodons, ground sloths, horses, and camels, along with birds and smaller mammals.[34]

To gain a better sense of the possible consequences of a large asteroid or comet impact, it could be helpful to consider an ancient and still more dramatic example. Thus, the Chicxulub Crater in the Yucatan provides a physical record of the climate catastrophe that followed an asteroid impact on earth 66 million years ago.[35]

> The event is blamed for the demise of three-quarters of plant and animal species, including the dinosaurs. The researchers' investigations suggest the impact threw more than 300 billion tonnes of sulphur into the atmosphere. This would have dropped temperatures globally below freezing for several years.[36]

The asteroid is thought to have been about 12 km in diameter in comparison to the Tunguska asteroid, which was about 50 m in diameter.[37]

As a final example of a biblically important asteroid impact, one might consider an event from the New Testament period. A recent discussion of this event has been given by Hartmann.[38] In the book of Acts there are three similar but not identical accounts of the journey of Saul of Tarsus (Paul) and a group of his friends from Jerusalem to Damascus. The purpose of their trip was to arrest Christians for violating religious traditions of the Jews. The accounts may be found in Acts 9:1-9, Acts 22:6-13, and Acts 26:12-20. Following are a few sentences selected from these sources that are intended to convey some of the main points.

> "Now as he (Saul) journeyed he approached Damascus, and suddenly a light from heaven flashed about him" (Acts 9:3). "As I (Saul) made my journey and drew near to Damascus, about noon a great light from heaven suddenly

shown about me" (Acts 22:6). "And when we had all fallen to the ground, I (Saul) heard a voice saying to me in the Hebrew language, 'Saul, Saul, why do you persecute me?' " (Acts 26:14). "Now those who were with me (Saul) saw the light but did not hear the voice of the one who was speaking to me" (Acts 22:9). "Saul arose from the ground; and when his eyes were opened, he could see nothing; so they led him by the hand and brought him into Damacus. And for three days he was without sight, and neither ate nor drank" (Acts 9:8-9).

In short, before Saul and his companions entered Damascus, they experienced a very bright light, and then a shock wave or earthquake that threw them all to the ground. Saul's position may have been more exposed than that of his companions. Thus, he was blinded while they weren't, and he distinctly heard a voice speaking to him that they seem not to have recognized. Today it seems natural to interpret the experience of Saul and his associates as being due to the impact of an asteroid. An interpretation of this sort in somewhat recent times was that of Baring-Gould.

> Whilst Saul was on his way to Damascus his miraculous conversion took place. Whereas to those who accompanied him the flash of light and crash that followed were an explosion of electic fire (lightning), or the fall of a meteorite, to Paul it was something much more.
> Of the certainty of his conviction that he both saw and heard Christ there can be no question. It was not the flash nor the sound that converted him, but the reality of the vision and the distinctness of the voice that spake. Once before, when a voice from heaven was heard, the people said "that it thundered," (John 12:29) and so doubtless did the guard, when they recovered from the shock.

8. Frequency of Impacts

We have three accounts of the conversion of St. Paul, and slight discrepancies exist between them, but so slight that it is puerile to make a point of the majority of them. If in one it is said that the soldiers heard no voice, or in another that they did, the reconciliation is obvious. They heard a sound, but did not distinguish articulate words.[39]

It may be observed that the earth has probably been subject to asteroid impacts since its creation far in the past. Impacts recorded in the Bible include the Old Testament incident leading to the destruction of Sodom and Gomorrah as discussed in Section 4. That event caused severe destruction east of the Dead Sea and the blinding of the residents of Sodom. The paragraphs above report another biblical impact. This New Testament example included the temporary blinding of Saul on the road to Damascus. There may have been other impacts in Bible times, but these two are clear examples for that era. It would seem that these events may also have been somewhat similar in magnitudes and consequences to the well-known Tunguska (30 June 1908) and Chelyabinsk (15 February 2013) incidents of modern times.

For the asteroid impact that led to the destruction of Sodom, it has been possible to estimate the impact date with a precision of about one year. It would, of course, be desirable to obtain comparable precision for the date of Paul's encounter with a blinding asteroid. Unfortunately, that has not yet been possible.

For times up to a few thousand years B.C., precise tree-ring dates can be obtained from the large boards and timbers used in the construction of buildings, ships, and other wooden structures. The tree-ring patterns embedded in such wooden materials record the occurrence of datable events such as volcanic eruptions and asteroid impacts. Unfortunately for this purpose, in the first centuries A.D. many building projects were based on stone, brick, or concrete materials. Such materials do not so readily preserve the precise dates of important climate events. They did, however, provide an unmatched degree of strength and durability.

> The ancient Romans were the first to mix sand and gravel with water and a bonding agent to make concrete. Although they called it *opus cementitium,* the bonding agent differed from that used in modern cement: it was a mixture of gypsum, quicklime, and pozzolana, a volcanic sand from Puteoli, near Mount Vesuvius, that made an outstanding material fit for massive vaults. Rome's Pantheon, completed in 126 C.E., still spans a greater distance than any other structure made of non-reinforced concrete.[40]

Actual historical writings often preserve date information, but such dates are typically of much poorer precision than those obtained by tree-ring methods (dendrochronology). Thus, uncertainty of several years may be unavoidable for the impact in the time of Paul.

> The first-century book, *Acts of the Apostles,* gives three separate descriptions of a bright light "from heaven," which occurred probably in the 30s (C.E.) near Damascus, Syria. The details offer a strikingly good match to a Chelyabinsk-class or Tunguska-class fireball. Among the most impressive, unexpected consistencies with modern knowledge is the first-century description of symptoms of temporary blindness caused by exposure to intense radiation, matching a condition now known as photokeratitis.[41]

8. Frequency of Impacts

It is also possible that some descriptions of the plagues reported in the biblical book Revelation may have reached the book's author John while he was writing in exile on the island of Patmos.[42] Thus, the asteroid-impact symbolism so evident in Revelation may have originated with the same impact event experienced by the apostle Paul on the road to Damascus.[43]

In conclusion, it may be noted again that many asteroids of various sizes and compositions have interacted with the earth throughout and previous to recorded history. Such interactions seem likely to continue in the future. Some of these events have been well documented in scientific studies, and two of them (in the Sodom and Damascus regions) are known from biblical texts.

1. L. W. Casperson, *Excursions in Biblical Chronology* (Lee Casperson, Ewing, NJ, 2018), Section 12.2, "From Noah to Abram," pp. 413-415; Table 12.1, p. 414.
2. Jubilees, (*The Books of Jubilees or The Little Genesis*, Translated from the Ethiopic Text by R. H. Charles, The McMillan Company, New York, 1917).
3. L. W. Casperson, *Excursions in Biblical Chronology*, op. cit., Section 13.2, "Chronology of the Hyksos era," pp. 445-451; Table 13.1, p. 447.
4. Jasher, (*The Book of Yashar*, M. M. Noah, Hermon Press, New York, 1972).
5. L. W. Casperson, *Patterns of Biblical Chronology* (Westbow Press, Bloomington, IN, 2012), Section 23.4, "Joseph and Apophis," pp. 575-581; Table 23.1, Chronology of Joseph, Apophis I, and Apophis II, p. 579.
6. Ibid., Section 20.6, The famine context, pp. 512-516 (2012); Table 20.1, Some biblical famines, p. 513; Chapter 21, Cause of the famine, pp. 523-542.
7. "Zoara," https://en.wikipedia.org/wiki/Zoara. Web. 9 August 2019.
8. This sculpture was originally entitled "Lot's Wife." It was created in 1962 by Anna Mahler, an Austrian sculptor who lived from 1904-1988. The sculpture was given to UCLA by Anna Bing Arnold in 1965, and it is on display in the Franklin D. Murphy Sculpture Garden.
9. M. Herbst (Hammer Museum, UCLA), private communcation, 17 October 2019.
10. G. A. Byers, "Those indefatigable Byzantines!," *Bible and Spade,* Volume 12, Number 3, pp. 81-85 (1999); p. 84.
11. *The Lost Books of the Bible and The Forgotten Books of Eden,* (The World Publishing Company, Cleveland and New York, 1927); 2 *Adam and Eve*, 19:8.
12. Ibid., 2 *Adam and Eve*, 20:31-32.
13. Ibid., 2 *Adam and Eve*, 20:34.

14. "Tunguska event," http://en.wikipedia.org/wiki/Tunguska event. Web. 9 August 2019.
15. P. J. Silva, T. E. Bunch, S. Collins, M. A. LeCompte, and A. West, "The 3.7 kaBP Middle Ghor Event: Catastrophic Termination of a Bronze Age Civilization," *Proceedings of the Annual Meeting of the American Schools of Oriental Research* (ASOR), Denver, Colorado, U.S.A., November 14-17, 2018, pp. 1-13; p. 1.
16. B. G. Wood, "The discovery of the sin cities of Sodom and Gomorrah," *Bible and Spade*, Volume 12, Number 3, pp. 66-80 (1999); "Looking for the sites," p. 67.
17. Ibid., "Means of the destruction of the cities of the plain," pp. 74-75.
18. Ibid., p. 75.
19. Ibid., p. 75.
20. Ibid., p. 75.
21. Ibid., p. 75.
22. C. L. Pearson, D. S. Dale, P. W. Brewer, P. I. Kuniholm, J. Lipton, S. W. Manning, "Dendrochemical analysis of a tree-ring growth anomaly associated with the Late Bronze Age eruption of Thera, *Journal of Archaeological Science*, Volume 36, pp. 1206-1214 (2009); p. 1211.
23. N. Platon, *Zakros, The Discovery of a Lost Palace of Ancient Crete* (Charles Scribner's Sons, New York, 1971).
24. Ibid., "Dating the Eruption," p. 276.
25. Ibid., pp. 278-279.
26. P. I. Kuniholm, M. W. Newton, C. B. Griggs, and P. J. Sullivan, "Dendrochronological dating in Anatolia: The second millennium BC," *Der Anschnitt, Anatolian Metal III*, Beiheft 18, pp. 41-47 (2005); p. 45
27. L. W. Casperson, *Patterns of Biblical Chronology*, op. cit., p. 535, Figure 21.1.
28. Santorini (Thera) Volcano, http://www.photovolcanica.com/VolcanoInfo/Santorini/Santorini.html. Web. 9 August 2019.
29. M. R. Rampino, "Reexamining Lyell's Laws," *American Scientist*, Volume 105, pp. 224-231, July-August 2017, pp. 229-230.

30. L. W. Casperson, *Excursions in Biblical Chronology*, op. cit., p. 306, Table 9.1.
31. Ibid., Chapter 9, "Evidence of the Biblical Flood," pp. 299-330.
32. D. W. Patten, *The Biblical Flood and the Ice Epoch* (Pacific Meridian Publishing Co., Seattle, Washington 98125, 1966), p. 153.
33. S. L. Vartanyan, Kh. A. Arslanov, T. V. Tertychnaya, and S. B. Chernov, "Radiocarbon dating evidence for mammoths on Wrangel Island, Artic Ocean, until 2000 B.C.," *Radiocarbon*, Volume 37, Number 1, pp. 1-6 (1995).
34. R. B. Firestone, A. West, J. P. Kennett, L. Becker, T. E. Bunch, Z. S. Revay, P. H. Schultz, T. Belgya, D. J. Kennett, J. M. Erlandson, O. J. Dickenson, A. C. Goodyear, R. S. Harris, G. A Howard, J. B. Kloosterman, P. Lechler, P. A. Mayewski, J. Montgomery, R. Poreda, T. Darrah, S. S. Que Hee, A. R. Smith, A. Stich, W. Topping, J. H. Wittke, and W. S. Wolbach, "Evidence for an extraterrestrial impact 12,900 years ago that contributed to the megafaunal extinctions and the Younger Dryas cooling," *Proceedings of the National Academy of Sciences of the United States of America*, Volume 104, Number 41, pp. 16016-16021 (9 October 2007), p. 16016.
35. L. W. Casperson, *Excursions in Biblical Chronology*, op. cit., p. 308.
36. J. Amos, "Asteroid impact plunged dinosaurs into catastrophic 'winter'," *Science & Environment,* http:www.bbc.com/news/science-environment-41825471. Web. 31 October 2017.
37. L. W. Casperson, *Excursions in Biblical Chronology*, op. cit., p. 306, Table 9.1.
38. W. K. Hartmann, "Chelyabinsk, Zond IV, and a possible first-century fireball of historical importance," *Meteoritics & Planetary Science*, Volume 50, Number 3, pp. 368-381 (2015).
39. S. Baring-Gould, *A study of St. Paul, his character and opinions* (Isbister and Co., Ltd., London, 1897), p. 82.

40. V. Smil, "Concrete Facts," *IEEE Spectrum,* March 2020, pp. 20-21, p. 21.
41. W. K. Hartmann, op. cit., p. 368.
42. L. W. Casperson, *Excursions in Biblical Chronology*, op. cit., Section 19.4, "Plagues of Revelation," pp. 704-707.
43. Ibid., Section 19.7, "An astrophysical possibility," pp. 721-723.